Beverages

Fancy Schmancy

Entertaining Made Easy!

Invitations
Party Favors
Decorations
Entertainment
Recipes

Printed in the United States of America
by G&R Publishing Co.

Distributed By:

507 Industrial Street
Waverly, IA 50677

ISBN 1-56383-197-X
Item #7058

Table of Contents

Yogurt Cooler

Makes 2 servings

1 (6 oz.) carton plain yogurt   **1 C. crushed ice**
1 C. frozen fruit (any kind)

In a blender, combine yogurt, frozen fruit and ice. Process at medium speed until well blended. Pour cooler into two medium glasses and serve.

Bailey's Blizzard

Makes 2 servings

2 oz. Bailey's Irish Cream   1 oz. brandy
2 oz. peppermint Schnapps   1 C. vanilla ice cream

    In a blender, combine Irish Cream liqueur, peppermint Schnapps, brandy and ice cream. Process at medium speed until well blended. Pour blizzard into two medium glasses and serve.

Tomato Juice Cocktail

Makes 2 servings

Ice cubes
2 C. tomato juice, divided
1 tsp. Worcestershire sauce,
    divided

2 tsp. lemon juice, divided
2 oz. vodka, divided
Salt and pepper

Fill two tall glasses with ice cubes. Pour 1 cup tomato juice over ice in each glass. Add 1/2 teaspoon Worcestershire sauce, 1 teaspoon lemon juice and 1 ounce vodka to each glass. Mix well and season with salt and pepper to taste.

Moon-Mint Cocktail

Makes 1 serving

2 C. milk   **1/4 tsp. mint extract**
2 T. chocolate syrup

In a blender, combine milk, chocolate syrup and mint extract. Process at medium speed until well blended. Pour cocktail into a medium glasses and serve.

Strawberry Fruit Smoothie

Makes 2 servings

1 banana   **1 C. sliced strawberries**
2 C. orange juice

Peel and slice the banana. In a blender, combine orange juice, banana and sliced strawberries. Process at medium speed until well blended. Pour smoothie into two medium glasses and serve.

Banana Slush Punch

Makes 25 (1 cup) servings

4 ripe bananas
2 C. sugar
6 C. water, divided
1 (46 oz.) can pineapple
    juice

2 (12 oz.) cans frozen orange
    juice concentrate
1 (12 oz.) can frozen lemonade
    concentrate
3 (1 liter) bottles ginger ale

Peel and slice the bananas. In a blender, combine bananas, sugar and 3 cups water. Blend until smooth. Pour mixture into a large bowl and stir in pineapple juice. Blend in orange juice concentrate, lemonade concentrate and remaining 3 cups water. Divide mixture into 3 plastic containers or pitchers and place in freezer until solid. Remove from freezer 3 to 4 hours before serving. Using one frozen portion at a time, place slush into a punch bowl and pour 1 liter ginger ale over slush mixture. When punch bowl is empty, replace with another container of slush mixture and another liter of ginger ale.

Chicago Lemonade

Makes 1 serving

1 lemon
1/2 C. water
1 T. sugar

1 oz. soda water
1 oz. 7-Up

In a tall glass, squeeze juice of lemon. Add water, sugar, soda water and 7-Up. Mix until well blended and sugar is completely dissolved. Garnish with fresh lemon peel.

Boston Iced Tea

Makes 14 servings

1 gallon water
1 C. sugar
15 tea bags

1 (12 oz.) can frozen
cranberry juice
concentrate

In a large pot over medium heat, place water. Bring water to a boil, add sugar and stir until sugar is completely dissolved. Add tea bags and let steep until tea reaches desired strength. Stir in cranberry juice concentrate, mixing until melted and well blended. Let cool before serving. Serve in tall glasses over ice.

Brandy Slush

Makes 24 servings

5 C. water
4 green tea bags
1 C. sugar
1 (16 oz.) can frozen
   lemonade concentrate
1 (16 oz.) can frozen
   orange juice concentrate
2 C. brandy
1 (2 liter) bottle lemon
   lime soda

In a large pot over medium heat, place water. Bring water to a boil and pour 2 cups boiling water into a separate pan. Add green tea bags to 2 cups water and let steep for 10 minutes. Meanwhile, pour remaining 3 cups water into a 9x13" baking dish. Stir sugar into boiling water in baking dish, mixing until sugar is completely dissolved. Add frozen lemonade and frozen orange juice concentrates and mix well. Add brandy and tea mixture. Stir and place in freezer overnight. To serve, using an ice cream scoop, scoop desired amount of brandy slush mixture into glasses and top with lemon lime soda.

Apple Tea Punch

Makes 2 servings

Ice cubes
2 C. brewed tea, divided

2 C. apple juice, divided
1 C. pineapple juice, divided

Fill two tall glasses with ice cubes. Let brewed tea cool to room temperature. Pour 1 cup brewed tea over ice in each glass. Add 1 cup apple juice and 1/2 cup pineapple juice to each glass. Mix well and serve.

Cranberry Cooler

Makes 1 serving

Ice
1/2 C. cranberry juice

1/4 C. grape juice
1/4 C. lemon lime soda

In a cocktail shaker with ice, add cranberry juice and grape juice and shake until well mixed. Strain mixture into a highball glass over ice and stir in lemon lime soda.

Cherry Cider

Makes 2 quarts

2 quarts apple cider
1 cinnamon stick

1 (3 oz.) env. cherry gelatin
  mix

In a large pot or saucepan over medium heat, place apple cider and cinnamon stick. Bring mixture to a boil, reduce heat and let simmer for 15 minutes. Stir in cherry gelatin and let simmer for 2 minutes, stirring constantly, until gelatin is completely dissolved. Ladle cider into mugs and serve warm.

Coffee Floats

Makes 4 servings

2 1/2 C. strong brewed coffee
2 tsp. sugar
2/3 C. half n' half

4 scoops vanilla or coffee
    flavored ice cream
1 (2 liter) bottle cola

In a large bowl, combine brewed coffee and sugar, mixing until sugar is completely dissolved. Stir in half n' half and mix well. Place 1 scoop of ice cream in each of four tall glasses and divide coffee mixture evenly between glasses. Fill each glass with cola.

Hot Mochas

Makes 4 servings

2 C. brewed coffee
1/3 C. cocoa powder
2 C. milk
1 T. sugar

1/2 tsp. vanilla
1/2 C. whipped topping,
    divided
Dash of cinnamon

   In a large saucepan over medium heat, place coffee, cocoa powder, milk and sugar. Heat mixture, stirring constantly, and bring to a simmer. Remove from heat and stir in vanilla. Pour mixture into four mugs and top each serving with 2 tablespoons whipped topping and a dash of cinnamon.

Spiced Café

Makes 8 servings

8 T. coffee granules
8 C. water
Peel of 1 orange

Peel of 1 lemon
30 cloves
4 tsp. sugar

In the filter basket of a coffee maker, place 1 filter. Place coffee granules, orange peel, lemon peel and cloves in filter. Add water to coffee maker and brew as usual. Place 1/2 teaspoon sugar in each of 8 mugs and pour brewed spiced coffee to fill each mug. Mix well, until sugar is dissolved, and serve warm.

Iced Cappuccino

Makes 3 servings

1 1/2 C. strong brewed coffee   **1/2 C. half n' half**
1/2 C. sweetened condensed   **1/2 tsp. vanilla**
   milk

In a medium bowl, combine brewed coffee and sweetened condensed milk. Using a whisk, mix until well blended. Whisk in half n' half and vanilla. Fill three tall glasses with ice and pour mixture over ice in each glass.

Cinnamon Hot Cocoa

Makes 4 servings

3 (1 oz.) squares unsweetened chocolate
1/2 C. sugar
1/4 C. coffee granules
1 tsp. cinnamon
1 1/2 C. water
4 C. milk
1/4 C. whipped topping, divided

Chop unsweetened chocolate squares into pieces. In a medium saucepan over medium heat, combine chopped chocolate, sugar, coffee granules, cinnamon and water. Heat mixture, until chocolate is melted, stirring constantly. Bring to a simmer for 4 minutes, stirring constantly. Stir in milk and continue to heat, being careful not to boil. Remove from heat and, using a whisk, stir thoroughly until frothy. Pour mixture into 4 mugs and top each serving with 1 tablespoon whipped topping.

Hors d'oeuvres

Cranberry Cheese Spread

Makes 24 servings

1 (16 oz.) can cranberry
    sauce
1 (4 oz.) can diced green
    chilies, drained
2 T. sliced green onions
1 T. lime juice

1/2 tsp. garlic salt
1/2 tsp. cayenne pepper
1/2 tsp. chili powder
1 (8 oz.) pkg. cream cheese,
    softened
Various crackers for dipping

In a medium bowl, combine cranberry sauce, drained chilies, green onions, lime juice, garlic salt, cayenne pepper and chili powder. Mix until well blended. To serve, place block of cream cheese on a serving dish and spoon 1 cup of the cranberry mixture over cream cheese. Serve with various crackers for dipping.

Monterey
Chip Dip

Makes 12 servings

1 (15 oz.) can pumpkin puree
1 (8 oz.) pkg. cream cheese,
    softened
1 (8 oz.) container sour
    cream
1 (4 oz.) can diced green
    chilies, drained
2 T. sliced jalapenos

1/4 tsp. garlic salt
1 medium tomato, seeded
    and chopped
1 (2 1/4 oz.) can sliced
    olives, drained
2 green onions, sliced
1/4 C. finely chopped red
    onions

In a medium bowl, combine pumpkin puree and cream cheese. Spread mixture evenly into the bottom of an 8" square baking dish. In a small bowl, combine sour cream, drained green chilies, sliced jalapenos and garlic salt. Spread sour cream mixture over pumpkin mixture in baking dish. Top with chopped tomatoes, sliced olives, sliced green onions and chopped red onions. Cover baking dish and refrigerate for 2 hours. Serve with tortilla chips for dipping.

Chocolate Fruit Kabobs

Makes 8 servings

1 C. chocolate chips
18 pieces of fresh fruit, such
    as strawberries, kiwi
    slices or pineapple chunks

6 (4") wooden skewers

Line a baking sheet with waxed paper. In a small bowl, place chocolate chips. Heat chocolate chips in microwave for 1 minute. Remove from microwave and mix until smooth, returning to microwave for 10 to 20 second intervals if necessary. Dip fruit pieces halfway into melted chocolate mixture and place on waxed paper. Place baking sheet with fruit in refrigerator for 5 to 10 minutes, until chocolate is hardened. Thread chocolate covered fruit pieces onto wooden skewers and serve.

Simple Fruit Tarts

Makes 15 tarts

1 (3 oz.) pkg. cream cheese, softened	1 (2 oz.) pkg. frozen mini phyllo dough shells, thawed
1/4 C. sour cream	Chopped assorted fruit*
1 T. orange juice	1/4 C. seedless strawberry jam
1/2 tsp. vanilla	

In a medium bowl, combine cream cheese, sour cream, orange juice and vanilla. Stir until well mixed. Spoon about 1 teaspoon of the cream cheese mixture into each phyllo shell. Top with chopped fruit. In a medium saucepan over medium heat, place strawberry jam. Heat until jam is melted and drizzle melted jam over fruit in each shell.

*Suggestions for chopped assorted fruit are: strawberries, raspberries, blueberries, kiwi, nectarines or crushed pineapple.

Mini Quiche

Makes 3 1/2 dozen

8 slices bacon
1/2 C. minced fresh
   mushrooms
1 T. butter
1/3 C. chopped green onions

1 2/3 C. shredded Swiss
   cheese
Pastry for 1 double crust pie
5 large eggs
1 2/3 C. sour cream

Preheat oven to 375°. On a lightly floured flat surface, roll pie pastry to 1/16" thickness. Using a 3" circle cutter, cut dough into 42 circles, re-rolling pastry scraps as needed. Fit each circle into the bottom and up sides of 2 1/2" muffin cups. Meanwhile, in a medium skillet over medium high heat, cook bacon until browned and crispy. Remove bacon to paper towels to drain. Crumble drained bacon into pieces. Drain skillet and place butter in skillet. When butter is melted, add minced mushrooms. Sauté mushrooms until softened. In a medium bowl, combine sautéed mushrooms, crumbled bacon, chopped green onions and shredded Swiss cheese. Mix well and divide filling evenly into pastry in muffin cups. In a large bowl, beat together eggs and sour cream, mixing until smooth. Spoon about 1 tablespoon over filling in each muffin cup. Bake in oven for 20 to 25 minutes. Remove from oven and let cool for 5 minutes. Gently lift quiche out of pan and serve warm.

Tortilla Ham Roll-Ups

Makes 12 to 16 servings

1 (8 oz.) pkg. cream cheese,
   softened
2 T. butter, softened
1 T. mixed herbs
4 (12") flour tortillas

1/2 lb. thinly sliced honey ham
1 (2 1/4 oz.) can chopped
   olives, drained
1 bunch green onions,
   finely chopped

In a small bowl, combine cream cheese and butter. Stir in mixed herbs and blend until well incorporated. Spread mixture evenly over each tortilla. Place slices of thin ham, chopped olives and chopped green onions over mixture on each tortilla. Starting at the edge of each tortilla, roll up tortilla tightly into a long roll. Place rolls on a plate and refrigerate for 1 hour. Remove from refrigerator and cut each roll into 1" slices before serving. Serve with toothpicks.

Party Turnovers

Makes 30 turnovers

1 lb. ground beef
1 (1 oz.) pkg. dry onion
  soup mix

1 C. shredded Cheddar cheese
3 (8 oz.) pkgs. refrigerated
  crescent rolls

Preheat oven to 375°. In a medium skillet over medium heat, cook ground beef until evenly browned. Drain skillet of fat and stir in onion soup mix and shredded Cheddar cheese. Separate crescent roll dough into individual triangles. Place 1 tablespoon of the meat and cheese mixture in the center of each triangle and fold one end over, sealing the filling inside. Place filled turnovers on an ungreased baking sheet and bake in oven for 15 minutes, until turnovers are golden brown.

Shrimp Wontons

Makes 60 wontons

1 C. cooked chopped shrimp
1 C. shredded coconut
1 (3 oz.) pkg. cream cheese,
    softened

1 (9 3/4 oz.) jar shrimp
    sauce, divided
60 won ton wrappers
1/4 C. honey

In a medium bowl, combine cooked chopped shrimp, shredded coconut, cream cheese and 1/2 cup shrimp sauce. Mix until well blended. Place about 2 teaspoons of the shrimp mixture onto one corner of each won ton wrapper. Moisten the edges of each wrapper with water and fold squares in half to form triangles. Press on the edges to seal the filling inside each won ton wrapper. Fill a large skillet with 1/4" vegetable oil. Place skillet over high heat and heat for 1 minute. Place filled won tons in hot oil for about 30 seconds on each side, flipping with a slotted spoon. When won tons are light golden brown, remove from skillet with slotted spoon and let drain on paper towels. In a small bowl, combine remaining shrimp sauce and honey. Mix well and serve won tons with sauce for dipping.

Zesty Crab Cakes

Makes 6 to 8 crab cakes

1 T. butter
1 onion, finely chopped
2 stalks celery, finely chopped
1 1/2 C. fresh or imitation
　chopped crab meat
2 C. dry bread crumbs,
　divided

1 (9 3/4 oz.) jar shrimp
　sauce, divided
1/2 C. shredded Monterey
　Jack cheese
1/4 C. sour cream
2 large eggs, lightly beaten
1/4 C. vegetable oil

In a large skillet over medium high heat, place butter. Heat until butter is melted and stir in chopped onion and chopped celery. Cook for about 3 to 5 minutes, stirring frequently, until vegetables are tender. In a large bowl, combine cooked onions and celery, chopped crab meat, 1 cup dry bread crumbs, 1/3 cup shrimp sauce, shredded Monterey Jack cheese, sour cream and beaten eggs. Mix until well incorporated and shape mixture into 2" round patties. Place remaining 1 cup dry bread crumbs in a shallow dish and coat crab cakes in bread crumbs. In same skillet, place 2 tablespoons vegetable oil. Heat oil and place half of the crab cakes in skillet, cooking on each side for 1 to 2 minutes, until golden brown. Remove crab cakes with a slotted spoon and let drain on paper towels. Repeat with remaining crab cakes, adding more oil to skillet if needed. Serve crab cakes with remaining shrimp sauce.

Fresh Veggie Squares

Makes 12 servings

1 (8 oz.) tube refrigerated
    crescent rolls
1 (8 oz.) pkg. cream cheese,
    softened
3/4 C. grated Parmesan
    cheese
3 T. ranch dressing

1/2 tsp. hot pepper sauce
1 C. halved cherry tomatoes
1 C. chopped red, yellow
    and/or green peppers
1 C. chopped broccoli florets
1/2 C. shredded carrots
Salt to taste

Preheat oven to 375°. Unroll crescent rolls on a non-stick baking sheet. Pinch dough together to make one 9x12" square of dough. Pinch 1/4" of dough around edges to make a rim in dough. Bake in oven for 12 to 14 minutes, until golden brown. Remove crust from oven and let cool on a wire rack. In a medium bowl, combine cream cheese, grated Parmesan cheese, ranch dressing and hot sauce. Mix well and spread over cooled crust. Over topping on crust, place one row of each chopped vegetable. Press down lightly on tomatoes, peppers, broccoli and carrots. If desired, sprinkle salt over veggies. Cut into 3" squares and serve immediately or chill in refrigerator, covered, for up to 3 days.

Mini Sausage Cheese Balls

Makes 30 servings

2 lbs. ground sausage
4 C. shredded sharp
   Cheddar cheese
1 1/2 C. Bisquick baking mix

1/2 C. chopped onions
1/2 C. chopped celery
1/2 tsp. garlic powder

    Preheat oven to 375°. In a medium bowl, combine ground sausage, shredded sharp Cheddar cheese, baking mix, chopped onions, chopped celery and garlic powder. Mix until well incorporated and shape mixture into 1" round balls. Place balls on an ungreased baking sheet and bake in oven for 15 minutes, until golden brown and sausage is cooked throughout. Serve immediately.

Ham & Swiss Bites

Makes 48 servings

1 C. shredded Swiss cheese
1/2 C. finely chopped
    cooked ham
1/3 C. mayonnaise

2 T. chopped green onions
1 T. horseradish sauce
48 rye bread chips or
    bagel chips

In a medium bowl, combine shredded Swiss cheese, finely chopped ham, mayonnaise, chopped green onions and horseradish sauce. Mix well and spread about 1 teaspoon of the cheese mixture over each rye chip. Place chips on a microwave-safe plate and heat for 10 to 15 seconds in microwave, until cheese begins to melt. Serve immediately.

Salmon Tea Sandwiches

Makes 12 servings

1/4 C. sour cream
1 (3 oz.) pkg. cream cheese, softened
2 tsp. fresh chopped dillweed
1 tsp. lemon juice

12 mini rye bread slices
1 medium cucumber, cut into 24 slices
6 smoked salmon slices, cut in half
Lemon peel for garnish

In a small bowl, combine sour cream, cream cheese, dillweed and lemon juice. Mix well and spread an even amount of the cream cheese mixture over each rye bread slice. Top each slice with 2 cucumber slices and 1 piece of smoked salmon. If desired, top mini sandwiches with a twist of lemon peel.

Spinach Artichoke Rolls

Makes 4 dozen

1 (17 1/2 oz.) pkg. frozen
   puff pastry
1 (10 oz.) pkg. frozen
   chopped spinach,
   thawed and drained
1 (14 oz.) can artichoke hearts,
   drained and chopped

1/2 C. mayonnaise
1/2 C. grated Parmesan cheese
1 tsp. onion powder
1 tsp. garlic powder
1/2 tsp. pepper

Let puff pastry sit at room temperature for 30 minutes. Meanwhile, in a medium bowl, combine drained spinach, chopped artichoke hearts, mayonnaise, grated Parmesan cheese, onion powder, garlic powder and pepper. Unfold one thawed pastry and place on a lightly floured flat surface. Spread 1/4 of the spinach mixture evenly over pastry, to within 1/2" of the edge. Roll up pastry into a roll, pressing down on edges to seal. Wrap roll in plastic wrap and place in freezer for 30 minutes. Repeat with remaining puff pastry sheets and spinach mixture. Preheat oven to 400°. Remove rolls from freezer and cut into 1/2" thick slices. Place slices, cut side down, on a baking sheet. Bake in oven for 20 minutes, or until golden brown.

Ribbon Tea Sandwiches

Makes 12 servngs

1/2 C. finely chopped
    cooked ham
1/4 C. mayonnaise, divided
2 T. sweet pickle relish
1/2 tsp. prepared mustard
2 hard-boiled eggs, chopped
2 T. finely chopped celery

1 (3 oz.) pkg. cream cheese,
    softened
1 tsp. fresh chopped parsley
1 tsp. fresh chopped green onion
8 slices whole wheat bread
8 slices white bread
1/4 C. butter, softened

In a small bowl, combine chopped cooked ham, 2 tablespoons mayonnaise, sweet pickle relish and prepared mustard. Mix well and set aside. In a separate bowl, combine chopped hard-boiled eggs, finely chopped celery and remaining 2 tablespoons mayonnaise. In a separate small bowl, combine cream cheese, chopped parsley and chopped green onions. Cut crusts from wheat and white bread slices and spread butter over one side of each slice of bread. Spread 2 tablespoons of the ham mixture over each of 4 slices of wheat bread. Top each slice with 1 slice of white bread. Spread 2 tablespoons of the egg mixture over those slices and top with remaining 4 slices of wheat bread. Spread about 1 tablespoon of the cream cheese mixture over those slices and top with remaining 4 slices of white bread. There should be four stacked sandwiches. Wrap sandwiches with plastic wrap and refrigerate for 1 hour. Before serving, cut each sandwich into thirds.

Cocktail Shrimp Dip

Makes 30 servings

1 (8 oz.) pkg. cream cheese, softened	2 tsp. lemon juice
2 C. frozen shrimp, thawed and chopped	1/4 tsp. garlic powder
1/4 C. finely chopped celery	1/8 tsp. onion salt
1/4 C. slivered almonds	1 (9 3/4 oz.) jar shrimp sauce
	Various crackers for dipping

In a medium bowl, combine cream cheese, chopped shrimp, finely chopped celery, slivered almonds, lemon juice, garlic powder and onion salt. Mix well and shape mixture into a ball. Place ball on a serving platter and refrigerate for 2 hours. Before serving, cover cheese ball with shrimp sauce. Serve with various crackers for dipping.

Walnut Stuffed Mushrooms

Makes 18 mushrooms

18 large mushrooms
1/4 C. chicken broth
1/4 C. chopped shallots
1 Roma tomato, diced
1/3 C. chopped walnuts

2/3 C. mayonnaise
1 1/2 C. dry bread crumbs
1 T. fresh chopped tarragon
   or 1 tsp. dried tarragon
Salt and pepper to taste

Preheat oven to 375°. Remove stems from mushroom caps. Chop mushroom stems and set aside. In a large skillet over medium high heat, place mushroom caps. Cook caps for about 1 minute on each side, until lightly browned. Place mushrooms, top side down, on a baking sheet. Return skillet to medium heat and add chicken broth. Bring to a boil and stir in chopped mushroom stems and chopped shallots. Cook for about 2 to 3 minutes, until most of the liquid has absorbed. Transfer mixture to a medium bowl and add diced tomatoes, chopped walnuts, mayonnaise, dry bread crumbs and tarragon. Mix well and season with salt and pepper to taste. Mound an even amount of the mixture into each mushroom cap. Bake in oven for 15 to 18 minutes. Serve warm.

Seafood Cocktail Toss

Makes 4 servings

1 lb. medium shrimp, cooked, peeled and deveined
3/4 C. Italian dressing
1 medium tomato, diced
1 (4 oz.) can diced green chilies, drained
1/3 C. chopped green onions
2 T. fresh chopped cilantro, optional
2 tsp. honey
1/8 tsp. hot pepper sauce

In a medium bowl, toss together cooked shrimp, Italian dressing, diced tomatoes, drained diced green chilies, chopped green onion, cilantro, honey and hot pepper sauce. Mix well and divide mixture into four cocktail or martini glasses. Chill in refrigerator at least 1 hour before serving.

Crispy Cheddar Rounds

Makes 4 dozen

3 slices bacon	1 tsp. Worcestershire sauce
1/2 C. butter, softened	1/8 tsp. salt
1 1/2 C. shredded Cheddar cheese	3/4 C. flour
	3/4 C. quick oats
3 T. water	Grated Parmesan cheese

In a small skillet over medium high heat, cook bacon until browned and crispy. Remove bacon to paper towels to drain. Crumble drained bacon into small pieces. In a medium bowl, combine butter, shredded Cheddar cheese, water, Worcestershire sauce and salt. Stir until well mixed and add flour, oats and crumbled bacon. Mix well and shape mixture into a 12" log. Cover log with plastic wrap and refrigerate for 4 hours. Preheat oven to 400°. Using a sharp knife, cut roll into 1/4" thick slices. Place rounds face-down, 1" apart on an ungreased baking sheet. Sprinkle tops of rounds lightly with grated Parmesan cheese. Bake in oven for 8 to 10 minutes, until lightly browned. Remove from oven and transfer immediately to wire racks to cool. Rounds are best when served warm.

Mini Party Pizzas

Makes 24 servings

24 whole wheat crackers
6 American cheese singles,
   quartered

2 to 4 T. pizza sauce
24 thin pepperoni slices

Preheat oven to 350°. Place whole wheat crackers in a single layer on a baking sheet. Place 1 cheese slice on each cracker and top with 1/4 teaspoon to 1/2 teaspoon pizza sauce. Place 1 pepperoni slice over pizza sauce on each cracker. Bake in oven for 3 to 5 minutes, until cheese is melted. Serve immediately.

Blue Cheese & Walnut Squares

Makes 12 to 16 servings

1 large pre-baked pizza crust
1 T. olive oil
1 tsp. balsamic vinegar

1 C. chopped walnuts
3/4 C. crumbled blue cheese
1/2 tsp. pepper

Preheat oven to 400°. Spray a baking sheet or pizza pan with non-stick cooking spray and place pre-baked pizza crust on pan. In a small bowl, whisk together olive oil and balsamic vinegar. Using a pastry brush, spread olive oil mixture over pizza crust. Sprinkle chopped walnuts, crumbled blue cheese and pepper evenly over pizza crust. Bake in oven for 15 minutes, until crust is golden brown and cheese is melted. Cut into squares and serve warm.

Desserts

Mixed Fruit Whip

Makes 4 to 6 servings

1 apple, finely chopped
2 pineapple rings, finely
    chopped
1 orange, peeled and
    chopped

1/2 C. cherries, finely chopped
Juice of 1 lemon
1 (14 oz.) can sweetened
    condensed milk
1 C. whipped topping

In a medium bowl, combine finely chopped apple, finely chopped pineapple, chopped oranges, finely chopped cherries and lemon juice. Set aside 2 tablespoons of the fruit mixture and place remaining fruit mixture in a blender. Add sweetened condensed milk and process until smooth. Transfer mixture to a medium bowl and fold in whipped topping and reserved 2 tablespoons fruit mixture. Spoon mixture into individual dessert cups and chill in refrigerator until ready to serve.

White Chocolate Cranberry Parfaits

Makes 6 servings

1 (16 oz.) can cranberry sauce
1 T. amaretto liqueur, optional
1 (3 1/3 oz.) pkg. instant vanilla or white chocolate pudding mix

1 C. milk
1 C. plus 6 T. whipped topping, divided

In a small bowl, combine cranberry sauce and amaretto liqueur. Mix well and set aside. In a small mixing bowl, combine pudding mix and milk at low speed for 30 seconds. Add 1 cup whipped topping and increase speed to medium for 2 to 3 minutes, or until soft peaks form. To assemble parfaits, into 6 serving glasses, spoon layers of the cranberry mixture followed by the pudding mixture. Chill in refrigerator for 15 minutes. Before serving, top each parfait with 1 tablespoon of the remaining whipped topping.

White Chocolate Dipped Fruit

Makes 24 servings

1 (6 oz.) box white baking
    bars, broken into pieces

1 T. margarine
24 pieces fresh fruit*

    Line a baking sheet with waxed paper. In a medium microwave-safe bowl, place broken white baking bars and margarine. Heat in microwave for 1 minute. Remove from microwave and stir until smooth. If necessary, return chocolate to microwave for 10 to 20 second intervals until completely melted and smooth. Dip fresh fruit pieces halfway into melted chocolate mixture and shake off excess. Set dipped chocolate pieces on prepared baking sheet and chill in refrigerator until chocolate is set.

*Some fresh fruit suggestions are: whole strawberries, orange slices, kiwi slices or banana pieces.

Poached Pears in Red Wine Sauce

Makes 6 servings

6 pears, peeled with stems
   still attached
1/2 C. sugar
2 C. red wine

1 cinnamon stick
Peel of 1 lemon
1 T. lemon juice
Peel of 1 lime, grated

In a medium saucepan over low heat, place peeled pears. Sprinkle sugar over pears and pour red wine into saucepan. Add cinnamon stick and lemon peel. Bring to a simmer for 10 to 15 minutes, being careful not to boil. Remove from heat and stir in lemon juice. Let pears cool while sitting in juice. To serve, place 1 pear in each of six serving bowls and top with some of the cooking juices from saucepan. Garnish with grated lime peel.

Raspberry Red Velvet Cake

Makes 9 servings

3 C. cake flour, sifted
2 T. cocoa powder
1 tsp. baking soda
1 tsp. baking powder
1/2 tsp. salt
1 2/3 C. sugar
1/2 C. butter, softened
4 large egg whites

2 C. buttermilk
1 (1 oz.) bottle red food
    coloring
2 tsp. vanilla, divided
1 (8 oz.) pkg. cream cheese,
    softened
2 3/4 C. powdered sugar
1/2 C. seedless raspberry jam

Preheat oven to 350°. Grease two 9" round cake pans and line bottoms of pans with waxed paper. In a medium bowl, combine sifted flour, cocoa powder, baking soda, baking powder and salt. In a medium mixing bowl, beat together sugar and butter at medium speed for 4 minutes. Add egg whites and continue to beat for 5 minutes, until mixture is fluffy. In a small bowl, using a whisk, combine buttermilk, food coloring and vanilla. Alternating, add flour mixture and buttermilk to butter mixture, stirring just until moistened. Pour batter into prepared pans. Bake in oven for 28 minutes, or until a toothpick inserted in center of cakes comes out clean. Remove from oven and let cakes cool in pans. Meanwhile, in a medium bowl, combine 1 teaspoon vanilla and cream cheese, mixing until smooth and fluffy. Add powdered sugar and mix just until blended. To assemble cake, place one baked cake layer on a serving platter. Top cake with raspberry jam and place remaining cake layer over jam. Spread frosting over top and sides of cake. Place cake in refrigerator until ready to serve.

Apple Fantasy

Makes 6 to 8 servings

2 eggs
1 C. sugar
1/2 C. brown sugar
3 tsp. vanilla, rum or
    bourbon

2/3 C. flour
3 tsp. baking powder
1/2 tsp. salt
3 C. diced apples
Vanilla ice cream

Preheat oven to 350°. In a medium mixing bowl, beat together eggs, sugar, brown sugar and vanilla. Add flour, baking powder and salt and mix until well incorporated. Fold in diced apples and spread mixture into a 9" square deep baking dish or soufflé dish. Bake in oven for 45 minutes. Serve warm with a scoop of vanilla ice cream.

Pralines &
Cream Cake

Makes 12 servings

1 (18 1/4 oz.) box white
  cake mix
3 eggs
1 C. coffee flavored liqueur
1/2 C. vegetable oil
1 C. butter, softened
1 C. brown sugar

1 1/2 C. chopped pecans
1 (3 1/3 oz.) pkg. instant
  vanilla pudding mix
1 1/2 C. milk
1 (8 oz.) pkg. cream cheese,
  softened
1 1/2 C. whipped topping

Preheat oven to 350°. Lightly grease a 9x13" baking dish and set aside. In a large mixing bowl, beat together white cake mix, eggs, liqueur and vegetable oil at medium speed for 2 minutes. Pour mixture into prepared pan. Bake in oven for 25 minutes, until a toothpick inserted in center of cake comes out clean. Remove cake from oven and let cool in pan on a wire rack. To make pralines, in a small saucepan over medium high heat, combine butter and brown sugar. Bring to a boil, stirring frequently, for 2 minutes. Remove from heat and stir in chopped pecans. Immediately pour mixture over cooled cake. Chill cake in refrigerator. Meanwhile, in a medium mixing bowl, combine instant vanilla pudding mix, milk, cream cheese and whipped topping at medium speed until well mixed. To serve, cut cake into squares and place one cake square on each serving plate. Top each serving with a dollop of the pudding mixture.

Simple
Strawberry
Triffle

Makes 8 servings

1/2 prepared angel food cake
2 C. whipped topping
2 (6 oz.) cartons strawberry
   yogurt

1 pint sliced strawberries
1/4 C. slivered almonds,
   toasted*

Tear angel food cake into 3/4" pieces and place half of the cake pieces into the bottom of a 2-quart serving bowl. Top with half of the whipped topping, 1 carton strawberry yogurt and half of the sliced strawberries. Repeat layers with remaining cake pieces, whipped topping, strawberry yogurt and sliced strawberries. Sprinkle slivered almonds over top of mixture. Refrigerate at least 2 hours before serving.
* To toast, place slivered almonds in a single layer on a baking sheet. Bake at 350° for approximately 10 minutes or until almonds are golden brown.

Chocolate Mousse

Makes 4 servings

1 C. chopped semi-sweet chocolate	1 tsp. instant coffee granules, optional
1/2 C. water	1 tsp. vanilla
5 eggs, separated	2 T. powdered sugar

In a small saucepan over low heat or double boiler, place chocolate and 2 tablespoons water. Meanwhile, in a medium bowl, using a whisk, beat egg yolks. Add beaten egg yolks and instant coffee granules to melted chocolate mixture and remove from heat. In a medium mixing bowl, beat egg whites, vanilla and powdered sugar until stiff peaks form. Slowly fold egg white mixture into melted chocolate mixture until well blended. Divide mousse into 4 individual serving bowls or champagne glasses and chill in refrigerator until mousse is thickened.

Cocoa Pumpkin Brownies

Makes 16 servings

2/3 C. brown sugar
1/2 C. pumpkin puree
1 large egg
2 large egg whites
2 T. vegetable oil
1 C. flour
1 tsp. baking powder

1 tsp. cocoa powder
1/2 tsp. cinnamon
1/2 tsp. allspice
1/4 tsp. salt
1/4 tsp. nutmeg
1/3 C. miniature chocolate
    chips

Preheat oven to 350°. Grease a 9" square baking dish and set aside. In a large mixing bowl, beat brown sugar, pumpkin puree, egg, egg whites and vegetable oil at medium speed until well blended. Stir in flour, baking powder, cocoa powder, cinnamon, allspice, salt and nutmeg. Beat at low speed until smooth. Stir in miniature chocolate chips and spread mixture evenly into prepared pan. Bake in oven for 15 to 20 minutes, or until a toothpick inserted in center of cake comes out clean. Remove from oven and let cool in pan. Cut into 2" brownies and serve.

Spiced Rum Crème Brulee

Makes 6 servings

2 C. liquid coffee creamer
1 T. cornstarch
2 tsp. flour
1/2 C. plus 3 T. sugar, divided
3 egg yolks
1 egg

2 T. spiced rum
2 tsp. vanilla
1/8 tsp. salt
1 (14 oz.) can sweetened
    condensed milk
1 T. brown sugar

Preheat oven to 325°. Place six 5-ounce ramekins in a baking dish. In a small saucepan over medium high heat, combine liquid coffee creamer, cornstarch and flour, whisking until cornstarch and flour are completely dissolved. Cook until mixture coats the back of a spoon and is the consistency of heavy cream. Remove from heat and let cool for 10 minutes. In a medium bowl, combine 1/2 cup sugar, egg yolks, egg, spiced rum, vanilla and salt. Using a whisk, blend until smooth and mix in sweetened condensed milk and cooled cream mixture. Strain mixture through a fine sieve and into prepared ramekins. Pour hot water into baking dish around ramekins to cover 3/4 of the way up each ramekin. Bake in oven for 45 minutes to 1 hour, or until custard is set. Remove from oven and remove ramekins from baking dish and chill in refrigerator for 4 hours or overnight. Preheat broiler. In a small bowl, combine brown sugar and remaining 3 tablespoons sugar. Sprinkle 2 teaspoons of the sugar mixture over custard in each ramekin. Place ramekins on a baking sheet and place under broiler until sugar is browned and slightly melted. Return to refrigerator for 1 hour to let the sugar harden.

Lemon Cookies

Makes about 2 dozen

1 lemon cake mix
1 egg
1 (8 oz.) container whipped
   topping

Powdered sugar

Preheat oven to 325°. In a large bowl, combine lemon cake mix, egg and whipped topping. Mix thoroughly until dough is sticky and stiff. Drop dough by teaspoonfuls into a small bowl of powdered sugar. Completely coat each cookie in powdered sugar and place on an ungreased baking sheet. Bake for no more than 8 to 10 minutes, being careful not to brown cookies. The cookies will be soft and crinkled on top when done. Immediately remove cookies from baking sheet and place on brown paper or a wire rack to cool.

Caramel Apple Quesadillas

Makes 10 servings

2 (12 oz.) pkgs. Stouffer's
    frozen harvest apples
1/4 C. sugar
1/4 tsp. cinnamon
4 T. butter

10 (6") flour tortillas
Caramel ice cream topping
Whipped topping, optional
Chopped almonds, optional

Prepare harvest apples according to package directions. In a small bowl, combine sugar and cinnamon. In a large skillet over medium low heat, place butter. Heat until butter is melted. Cook tortillas in skillet, one at a time, for 3 minutes on each side, until golden. Sprinkle heated tortillas with sugar and cinnamon mixture and keep warm until all tortillas are heated. Place tortillas on a cutting board and top with some of the harvest apples mixture. Fold each tortilla over and cut in half. Place on a serving plate and drizzle caramel ice cream topping over quesadillas. If desired, top with whipped topping and chopped almonds.

Chocolate Almond Coffee Cake

Makes 12 servings

1/2 C. chopped almonds, toasted*
1/3 C. brown sugar
1/4 C. chocolate chips
1 T. cocoa powder
1 T. instant coffee granules
1 1/2 tsp. chopped dried apricots
3/4 tsp. cinnamon

2 3/4 C. flour
1 1/2 tsp. baking powder
1 1/2 tsp. baking soda
1/2 tsp. salt
3/4 C. butter, softened
1 1/2 C. sugar
1 tsp. vanilla
3 large eggs
2 C. plain yogurt

Preheat oven to 350°. Grease a 10" bundt pan or 9x13" baking dish. In a medium bowl, combine toasted almonds, brown sugar, chocolate chips, cocoa powder, instant coffee granules, chopped apricots and cinnamon. Mix well and set aside. In a separate bowl, combine flour, baking powder, baking soda and salt. In a large mixing bowl, beat butter until lightened and fluffy. Add sugar and vanilla and beat for 2 minutes. Add eggs, one at a time, beating well after each addition, until mixture is smooth. Alternating, add flour mixture and yogurt to butter mixture. Pour half of the batter into prepared pan and top with half of the almond mixture. Repeat layers with remaining batter and remaining almond mixture. Bake in oven for 1 hour, or until a toothpick inserted in center of cake comes out clean. Let cool on a wire rack for 10 minutes before inverting cake onto serving plate.
* To toast, place chopped almonds in a single layer on a baking sheet. Bake at 350° for approximately 10 minutes or until almonds are golden brown.

Caramel Pecan Cheesecake

Makes 8 servings

2 C. vanilla wafer cookie crumbs
6 T. butter or margarine, melted
1 (14 oz.) bag caramels, unwrapped
1 (15 oz.) can evaporated milk

1 C. chopped pecans
2 (8 oz.) pkgs. cream cheese, softened
1/2 C. sugar
2 eggs
1/2 C. chocolate chips, melted
1 tsp. vanilla

Preheat oven to 350°. In a medium bowl, combine cookie crumbs and melted butter. Mix well and spread mixture into the bottom and up sides of a 9" springform pan. Bake in oven for 10 minutes. In a medium microwave-safe bowl, place caramels and evaporated milk. Heat in microwave for 4 to 5 minutes, stirring after every 1 minute, until melted. Pour melted caramel mixture over baked crust and top with chopped pecans. In a small mixing bowl, beat together cream cheese and sugar. Add eggs, one at a time, beating well after each addition. Blend in melted chocolate chips and vanilla. Pour mixture over pecans in baked crust. Place springform pan on a baking sheet. Bake in oven for 45 minutes. Before serving, loosen cake from rim of pan.

Apple Coffee Cake with Brown Sugar Sauce

Makes 1 (9") cake

2 to 3 small apples
2 1/2 C. flour
1 1/2 C. brown sugar
3/4 C. butter or margarine,
    softened
1 C. chopped walnuts,
    toasted*

1 tsp. baking soda
1 tsp. cinnamon
1/2 tsp. salt
1 egg, lightly beaten
3/4 C. sour cream
1 tsp. vanilla

Preheat oven to 375°. Grease a 9" round or springform pan. Peel, core and chop the apples and set aside. In a large bowl, combine flour, brown sugar and butter with a fork until mixture resembles coarse crumbs. Mix in chopped walnuts and place half of the crumbly mixture into a prepared springform pan. To remaining half of the crumb mixture add baking soda, cinnamon and salt. Make a well in the center of the mixture and add egg, sour cream and vanilla to well. Mix until smooth and add flour mixture, stirring until well combined. Fold in chopped apples. Pour batter over crumb mixture in springform pan. Bake in oven for 1 hour and 20 minutes, or until a toothpick inserted in center of cake comes out clean.

* To toast, place chopped walnuts in a single layer on a baking sheet. Bake at 350° for approximately 10 minutes or until walnuts are golden brown.

Coconut Macaroons

Makes 2 dozen

1 (14 oz.) pkg. shredded
   coconut
1 (14 oz.) can sweetened
   condensed milk

2 tsp. vanilla
1 tsp. almond extract

Preheat oven to 350°. Grease a baking sheet and set aside. In a large bowl, combine shredded coconut, sweetened condensed milk, vanilla and almond extract. Mix well and drop mixture by teaspoonfuls onto prepared baking sheet. Press each cookie lightly with the back of a spoon. Bake in oven for 10 to 14 minutes or until lightly browned around the edges. Immediately remove macaroons from oven and place on wire racks to cool.

Truffle Fudge Cheesecake

Makes 8 servings

2 C. chocolate chips	4 eggs
3 (8 oz.) pkgs. cream cheese, softened	2 tsp. vanilla
1 (14 oz.) can sweetened condensed milk	1 prepared Oreo crumb pie crust

Preheat oven to 300°. In a medium saucepan or double boiler over low heat, place chocolate chips. Heat chocolate chips, stirring constantly, until melted. In a large mixing bowl, beat cream cheese until fluffy. Add sweetened condensed milk and stir until smooth. Mix in melted chocolate, eggs and vanilla. Mix well and pour mixture into prepared pie crust. Bake in oven for 1 hour and 5 minutes, or until center of cheesecake is set.

Lemon Bars

Makes 2 dozen

2 C. plus 1 T. flour, divided
1/2 C. powdered sugar
1 C. butter or margarine,
    softened
1 (14 oz.) can sweetened
    condensed milk
4 large eggs
2/3 C. lemon juice

1 tsp. baking powder
1/4 tsp. salt
4 drop yellow food coloring,
    optional
1 T. grated lemon peel
Additional powdered sugar
    for dusting

Preheat oven to 350°. In a medium bowl, combine 2 cups flour and 1/2 cup powdered sugar. Using a pastry blender, cut in butter until mixture resembles fine crumbs. Press mixture into bottom and halfway up sides of a 9x13" baking dish. Bake in oven for 20 minutes. In a large mixing bowl, combine sweetened condensed milk and eggs at medium speed until fluffy. Beat in lemon juice, remaining 1 tablespoon flour, baking powder, salt and food coloring just until blended. Fold in grated lemon peel and pour mixture over baked crust. Return to oven for an additional 20 to 25 minutes, or until filling is set and crust is golden brown. Remove from oven and let cool on a wire rack before cutting into bars. Chill in refrigerator for 2 hours. Before serving, dust tops of bars with additional powdered sugar.

Mudslide Pie

Makes 8 servings

1 prepared Oreo crumb
  pie crust
1 C. chocolate chips
1 tsp. instant coffee
  granules
1 tsp. hot water
3/4 C. sour cream
1/2 C. sugar

1 tsp. vanilla
1 1/2 C. heavy whipping
  cream
1 C. powdered sugar
1/4 C. cocoa powder
2 T. miniature chocolate
  chips

In a double boiler over low heat, place chocolate chips. Heat until chocolate is melted and smooth, stirring frequently. Remove from heat and let cool for 10 minutes. In a medium bowl, combine instant coffee granules and hot water. Add sour cream, sugar and vanilla and mix until sugar is completely dissolved. Stir in melted chocolate and mix until smooth. Spread mixture into prepared crust and chill in refrigerator. In a small mixing bowl, beat heavy whipping cream, powdered sugar and cocoa powder at high speed until stiff peaks form. Spread mixture over chilled chocolate layer in crust. Sprinkle miniature chocolate chips over pie and place in freezer for 6 hours or until firm.

Cinnamon Chocolate Pudding

Makes 8 servings

1/2 C. sugar
2 T. cornstarch
1 tsp. cinnamon
2 (12 oz.) cans evaporated
   milk

1 C. chocolate chips
2 egg yolks, lightly beaten
1/2 C. shredded coconut

In a large saucepan over medium heat, combine sugar, cornstarch and cinnamon. Gradually stir in evaporated milk, chocolate chips and beaten egg yolks. Bring to a boil, stirring constantly, until mixture is thickened and chocolate is melted. Pour chocolate mixture into 8 individual serving cups. Chill in refrigerator for 1 hour and sprinkle shredded coconut over top.

Chocolate Praline Tart

Makes 12 servings

1 1/2 C. flour
3/4 C. powdered sugar
1/2 C. cocoa powder
1 tsp. vanilla
1 tsp. salt
2 2/3 C. butter, divided

1 1/2 C. brown sugar
2/3 C. honey
1/4 C. sugar
3 C. pecan halves
1/3 C. heavy whipping cream

Preheat oven to 350°. In a food processor or blender, combine flour, powdered sugar, cocoa powder, vanilla and salt. Process on high until well blended. While still blending, gradually add 1 2/3 cups butter, a few tablespoons at a time. Process until dough forms a ball on top of the blades. Press dough into the bottom and up sides of a 12" springform pan. Bake in oven for 10 minutes or until lightly browned. Set aside to cool. Meanwhile, in a large saucepan over medium high heat, combine remaining 1 cup butter, brown sugar, honey and sugar. Bring to a boil. Boil for 3 minutes and stir in pecan halves and whipping cream. Return to a boil and immediately pour mixture into cooled crust. Bake in oven for 20 minutes, until center of tart is bubbling. Let cool for 2 hours.

Almond Chocolate Ice Cream Roll

Makes 8 servings

1/3 C. flour
1/4 C. cocoa powder
1 tsp. baking powder
1/4 tsp. salt
4 large eggs, separated
1/2 tsp. vanilla
1 1/4 C. plus 1/3 C. sugar, divided

Powdered sugar
1 quart butter almond or chocolate almond ice cream, softened
1 (12 oz.) pkg. frozen raspberries, thawed
1 tsp. lemon juice

Preheat oven to 375°. Grease a 10x15" jellyroll pan. In a medium bowl, combine flour, cocoa powder, baking power and salt. Mix well and set aside. In a small mixing bowl, beat together egg yolks and vanilla at high speed for 5 minutes. Gradually add 1/3 cup sugar and beat for an additional 5 minutes, until sugar is dissolved. In a large mixing bowl, beat egg whites at medium speed until soft peaks form. Gradually add 1/2 cup sugar and beat at high speed until stiff peaks form. Sprinkle flour mixture over egg white mixture and mix just until blended. Spread mixture into prepared pan. Bake in oven for 12 to 15 minutes, or until top springs back when lightly touched. Remove from oven and immediately loosen edges of cake from pan. Sprinkle a large kitchen towel with powdered sugar and invert cake onto towel. Roll up cake in towel, starting at one of the short ends. Let cool on a wire rack. Unroll cake and spread softened ice cream to within 1" of the edges. Re-roll cake without towel, wrap in aluminum foil and place in freezer for 1 hour. In a blender, place thawed raspberries. Process until smooth. Strain blended raspberries through a fine-hole sieve to remove seeds. In a small saucepan over medium heat, combine raspberry puree, lemon juice and remaining 3/4 cup sugar. Bring to a boil for 3 minutes, stirring constantly. To serve, slice frozen ice cream roll into 8 slices and place on dessert plates. Spoon raspberry sauce over each serving.

Mini Treasure Raspberry Cakes

Makes 10 servings

3/4 C. sugar
1/2 C. butter, softened
2 large eggs
1/4 C. evaporated milk
1 tsp. vanilla
1 C. flour

1/4 tsp. salt
1 C. fresh raspberries
10 Nestle Chocolate Crème
    Signatures Treasures
Powdered sugar

Preheat oven to 350°. Grease 10 muffin cups or fill with paper liners. In a large mixing bowl, beat together sugar and butter at medium speed until well mixed. Add eggs, evaporated milk and vanilla and continue to beat until blended. Stir in flour and salt and gently fold in raspberries. Pour most of the batter evenly into prepared muffin cups. Place 1 Chocolate Crème Signatures Treasures over batter in each cup, pressing down lightly. Spoon remaining batter over chocolate in each muffin cup, covering the Signatures Treasures completely. Bake in oven for 20 to 22 minutes, or until cakes are golden brown and top is set. Remove from oven and let cool in pan for 10 minutes. Gently release muffins from cups and invert onto serving plates. Sprinkle with powdered sugar and serve warm.

Cappuccino Oreo Triffle

Makes 8 servings

1/2 C. sugar
1/4 C. cornstarch
1 T. instant coffee granules
1 large egg

2 1/2 C. milk
1 T. Kahlua
16 Oreo cookies, divided
1 1/2 C. whipped topping

In a large bowl, using a whisk, combine sugar, cornstarch, instant coffee granules and egg. In a heavy saucepan over medium high heat, place milk. Cook milk until tiny bubbles appear around the edge of the saucepan, being careful not to boil. Gradually pour hot milk into egg mixture, stirring constantly with a whisk. Return milk mixture to saucepan and place over medium heat until thickened, about 3 minutes, stirring constantly. Reduce heat to low and continue to cook for 2 minutes. Remove from heat and mix in Kahlua. Fill a large bowl with ice. Pour mixture into a medium bowl and place bowl inside large bowl with ice, stirring constantly until mixture cools. Coarsely chop 8 Oreo cookies and fold into the pudding mixture. Into 8 parfait cups, spoon about 1/2 cup of the pudding mixture. Cover parfait cups and chill in refrigerator for 2 hours. Before serving, top each serving with 1 of the remaining Oreo cookies. Serve cold.

Invitations

Matchbook
Invites

Makes 2 invites

1 sheet of 8 1/2x11" paper
Staples
Markers or colored pens

Cut the 8 1/2x11" sheet of paper in half to make two sheets that are 5 1/2x8 1/2". Fold the short end of each piece of paper up 1". Fold the top of the sheet of paper down 3 1/2" from the top (Diagram 1). Place a staple within the 1" section and decorate the inside of the invite as desired. Fold down the top of the invite and slip inside the stapled section, just like a matchbook. Address the outside of the matchbook and mail to your guests. Don't forget the stamp!

Diagram 1

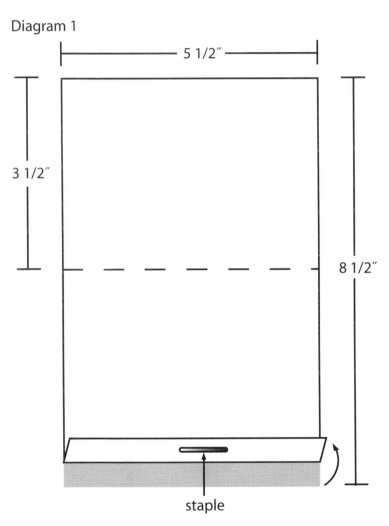

5 1/2″

3 1/2″

8 1/2″

staple

Dress Shirt Invite

Makes 1 invite

1 sheet of 8 1/2x11" paper
Additional paper for decoration
Glue
Markers or colored pens

Place the paper face-down in front of you and fold in half vertically. Unfold the paper. Line up the left and right sides of the paper with the centerfold and crease (Diagram 1). Unfold the paper and lay flat once again. Fold the top left and right corners in to line up with the outer crease on either side, forming little triangles. Using your index finger and thumb, pinch together the outside points of each triangle so they meet, and crease (Diagram 2). While pinching triangles, fold down the top edge to make the sleeves (Diagram 3). Turn paper upside down and flip over. Fold down the top edge 3/4" to make the collar (Diagram 4). Turn paper over again and fold down the top left and right corners to meet at the center (Diagram 5). Fold the bottom end of the sheet up and tuck the shirt under the edges of the collar (Diagram 6). If desired, cut out decorations, such as a necktie, necklace, flowers, etc., and glue them onto front of the shirt. Open the shirt and personalize with greetings and party information. Address the back of the shirts, add a stamp and place in the mailbox for your guests.

70

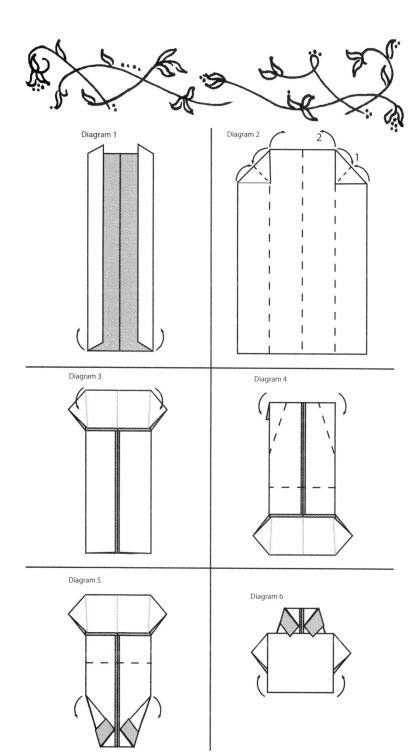

Diagram 1

Diagram 2

Diagram 3

Diagram 4

Diagram 5

Diagram 6

Satin Ribbon Invites

Makes 2 invites

1/8" hole punch
Satin ribbon
2 A7 envelopes
2 5x7" sheets cardstock
1 sheet of 8 1/2x11" vellum paper

Write up the invitation exactly as you want it printed in a word processing program of a computer. Copy and paste the text so that it fits twice on one sheet of paper. Print the text on the sheet of vellum paper. Be careful not to touch the ink, as it takes a few minutes to dry on vellum paper. Cut the two sections of text apart and carefully tear the bottom side of each sheet for a torn-effect. Place one sheet of vellum over each sheet of cardstock and match up the sheets at the top edge. Punch two holes 1" apart through both the vellum sheet and the cardstock. Thread the satin ribbon through both holes from the back and tie a bow at the top of the invite, securing the vellum sheet to the cardstock. Address the envelopes and place one invite inside each envelope, add a stamp and place in the mailbox for your guests.

Please join us...
Red Hat Party!
Tuesday, May 1
7:00 p.m.
Judy's House
5 1 5 Main St.

Silver Tube Invites

Cardstock
Marker or colored pens
Silver mailing tube*
Wrapped miniature chocolates
Confetti

Write the invitation by hand on cardstock. Be sure to include details like What, When, Where, Why and Who to R.S.V.P. Roll up the invite and place inside a silver mailing tube. Fill the tube with wrapped chocolates, confetti or other little gifts to entice your guests or coordinate with the theme of your party. Close the tube and affix a mailing label and stamp directly to the outside of the tube. Check at the post office to confirm the correct amount of postage. Place the tube directly in the mailbox to send to your guest.
*Mailing tubes are available at most packaging and stationery stores.

Mary Pendergrass
110 Main Street SE
Your Town, USA
00010

75

Tea Party Box

Makes 1 invite

1 bracelet-size gift box
1 tea bag
Black marker
Tape

You'd be surprised by how many "objects" can be mailed other than just letters. To make a mini party box invitation, write the invite directly inside the bottom piece of a bracelet-size gift box. If this is too difficult, write the invite on a small piece of paper, fold and place inside the gift box. If you are having a tea party, place a tea bag or other appropriate gift inside the box to entice your guests. For a Christmas party, place a small ornament or wrapped piece of chocolate inside the box. For a cocktail party, write the invite on a cocktail napkin, fold and place inside the box. For a festive fall party, place colored fall leaves inside the box with the invite. Close the box with the lid and tape closed. Attach a mailing label and stamp to the top of the box and place in the mailbox for your guests.

Mary Pendergrass
110 Main Street SE
Your Town, USA
00010

37¢

Tea Party! Y

TEA

77

E-Mail Invites

Not all party invitations need to be sent through postal mail. If you and all your guests have computers and e-mail addresses, sending invites via cyberspace is a great way to save time and money! There are many websites that offer free web-invites or e-cards that can be personalized and sent directly to the recipient's e-mail inbox. Some sites will require you to become a member before sending their cards. In almost all cases, these memberships are free. A lot of these sites offer cute animations or music to send, as well. Some great websites to help you personalize and send your e-mail invites are:

- www.bluemountain.com
- www.e-cards.com
- www.hallmark.com
- www.123greetings.com
- www.yahoo.americangreetings.com

Entertainment

Blitz

1 deck of cards
2 to 9 players

The object of this game is to collect cards in a single suit that have a sum of 31 points. Determine which player is the dealer. Have the dealer deal three cards, face-down, to each player. The dealer sets all remaining cards in the deck face-down in the center of the table and turns the first card face-up to start the discard pile. The players can pick up their cards and look at them. Any cards of the same suit can be matched up, trying to get the most number of points. Aces are worth 11 points and face cards are worth 10 points. The first player to the left gets to choose whether they want to keep all of their dealt cards, take the face-up card from the discard pile or choose a new card from the face-down pile. All players can have only 3 cards in their hand. So, if a player decides to take a new card, they have to discard 1 card at the same time to the face-up pile. Play continues around the table until a player has three cards that add up to 31 points, or if that player believes they have the highest number of points in the group. A player can indicate that they want to stop play and show their cards at any time by knocking on the table. When a player knocks on the table, all remaining players get one final turn to try to increase their total. After all players have had a final turn, all players turn over their cards. The player with the most cards of the same suit that add up to the highest number is the winner.

King's Corners

1 deck of cards
2 or more players

The object of the game is to be the first person to get rid of all your cards. Determine which player is the dealer. Have the dealer deal seven cards to each player. Place the rest of the cards face-down in the center of the table. The dealer then turns over the four top cards, laying one card face-up spreading from each side of the deck. Each player must pick up one card from the center pile at the beginning of each turn. The first player to the left has a turn to try to get rid of some of her cards by laying them on the face-up piles. If a player has a King, the King can be placed face-up at a diagonal (in the corners) from the center pile. A card can be laid on the face-up piles if it is in descending order and the opposite color of the face-up card. For example, only a red Queen can be laid on a black King, only a red 6 can be placed on a black 7, only a black Ace can be set on a red 2. An entire line of descending cards can be moved to another line if the first (the bottom card) in the pile would be correctly placed in order on another line. When an entire line is moved, creating an open space, that player can place any card from her hand in that space. A player can continue her turn as long as she has cards to lie down. The first player to lay down all of her cards is the winner.

Draw Dominoes

1 set of Dominoes
2 or more players

Find the Domino tile that has double 6 on the face and place it face up in the playing area. Set all Dominoes face-down on the table. Have each player select six or seven Dominoes from the pile. The more players you have, the fewer Dominoes they should take from the pile. If you have more than four players, have each player take six Dominoes. If you have more than seven players, have each player take five Dominoes. Determine which player will go first. Each player gets a chance to lay down one tile that matches up in the line. Doubles are placed crosswise on the line. If the player does not have a tile that matches with any open end in the line, they have to pick up another Domino from the face-down pile. The first player to get rid of all their Dominoes is the winner.

Crazy Eights

1 deck of cards
2 or more players

The object of the game is to be the first person to get rid of all your cards. Determine which player is the dealer. Have the dealer deal seven cards to each player. Place the rest of the cards face-down in the center of the table. The dealer then turns over the first card, laying that card face-up on the table. If that card is an 8, place that card back into the pile and turn over the next card. The first player to the left has a chance to discard one of their cards. The player can discard a card only if it is the same suit or number of the face-up card. After a player has discarded one card, her turn is over. If she doesn't have a card that can be discarded, that player has to draw from the face-down pile and her turn is over. An 8 can be used as a wild card at any time. The first player to lay down all of her cards is the winner.

1000 Dice

1 deck of cards
2 or more players
Five dice

The object of the game is to be the first player to reach a score of 1000. To start, have each player roll one dice. The player with the highest roll gets to go first and play will continue clockwise from that player. On each turn, the player rolls all five dice at once. Any dice that show a one are worth 100 points. Any dice that show a five are worth 50 points. All other dice are not worth any points, unless there are a multiple dice showing that number. If multiple dice are showing the same number, the player gets 100 times the number on that dice. For example, if a player rolls a one, a five and three twos, they would get 100, 50 and 200 points for a total of 350 points. If the player has not scored any points, their turn is over and it is the next player's turn. However, if the player has scored points on a roll, they can decide to either keep the points and end their turn or continue to roll to try to get more points. If the player gets more points on the next roll, it is added to her total, however, if she does not get any points on her next roll, her turn is over and she loses all of her points. Have someone record the points for each round throughout the game. The first player to score 1000 points is the winner.

84

Mary Pendergrass
110 Main Street SE
Your Town, USA
00010

37¢

Tea Party! Y

TEA

E-Mail Invites

Not all party invitations need to be sent through postal mail. If you and all your guests have computers and e-mail addresses, sending invites via cyberspace is a great way to save time and money! There are many websites that offer free web-invites or e-cards that can be personalized and sent directly to the recipient's e-mail inbox. Some sites will require you to become a member before sending their cards. In almost all cases, these memberships are free. A lot of these sites offer cute animations or music to send, as well. Some great websites to help you personalize and send your e-mail invites are:

- **www.bluemountain.com**
- **www.e-cards.com**
- **www.hallmark.com**
- **www.123greetings.com**
- **www.yahoo.americangreetings.com**

Entertainment

Blitz

1 deck of cards
2 to 9 players

    The object of this game is to collect cards in a single suit that have a sum of 31 points. Determine which player is the dealer. Have the dealer deal three cards, face-down, to each player. The dealer sets all remaining cards in the deck face-down in the center of the table and turns the first card face-up to start the discard pile. The players can pick up their cards and look at them. Any cards of the same suit can be matched up, trying to get the most number of points. Aces are worth 11 points and face cards are worth 10 points. The first player to the left gets to choose whether they want to keep all of their dealt cards, take the face-up card from the discard pile or choose a new card from the face-down pile. All players can have only 3 cards in their hand. So, if a player decides to take a new card, they have to discard 1 card at the same time to the face-up pile. Play continues around the table until a player has three cards that add up to 31 points, or if that player believes they have the highest number of points in the group. A player can indicate that they want to stop play and show their cards at any time by knocking on the table. When a player knocks on the table, all remaining players get one final turn to try to increase their total. After all players have had a final turn, all players turn over their cards. The player with the most cards of the same suit that add up to the highest number is the winner.

King's Corners

1 deck of cards
2 or more players

The object of the game is to be the first person to get rid of all your cards. Determine which player is the dealer. Have the dealer deal seven cards to each player. Place the rest of the cards face-down in the center of the table. The dealer then turns over the four top cards, laying one card face-up spreading from each side of the deck. Each player must pick up one card from the center pile at the beginning of each turn. The first player to the left has a turn to try to get rid of some of her cards by laying them on the face-up piles. If a player has a King, the King can be placed face-up at a diagonal (in the corners) from the center pile. A card can be laid on the face-up piles if it is in descending order and the opposite color of the face-up card. For example, only a red Queen can be laid on a black King, only a red 6 can be placed on a black 7, only a black Ace can be set on a red 2. An entire line of descending cards can be moved to another line if the first (the bottom card) in the pile would be correctly placed in order on another line. When an entire line is moved, creating an open space, that player can place any card from her hand in that space. A player can continue her turn as long as she has cards to lie down. The first player to lay down all of her cards is the winner.

Draw Dominoes

1 set of Dominoes
2 or more players

Find the Domino tile that has double 6 on the face and place it face up in the playing area. Set all Dominoes face-down on the table. Have each player select six or seven Dominoes from the pile. The more players you have, the fewer Dominoes they should take from the pile. If you have more than four players, have each player take six Dominoes. If you have more than seven players, have each player take five Dominoes. Determine which player will go first. Each player gets a chance to lay down one tile that matches up in the line. Doubles are placed crosswise on the line. If the player does not have a tile that matches with any open end in the line, they have to pick up another Domino from the face-down pile. The first player to get rid of all their Dominoes is the winner.

Crazy Eights

1 deck of cards
2 or more players

The object of the game is to be the first person to get rid of all your cards. Determine which player is the dealer. Have the dealer deal seven cards to each player. Place the rest of the cards face-down in the center of the table. The dealer then turns over the first card, laying that card face-up on the table. If that card is an 8, place that card back into the pile and turn over the next card. The first player to the left has a chance to discard one of their cards. The player can discard a card only if it is the same suit or number of the face-up card. After a player has discarded one card, her turn is over. If she doesn't have a card that can be discarded, that player has to draw from the face-down pile and her turn is over. An 8 can be used as a wild card at any time. The first player to lay down all of her cards is the winner.

1000 Dice

1 deck of cards
2 or more players
Five dice

The object of the game is to be the first player to reach a score of 1000. To start, have each player roll one dice. The player with the highest roll gets to go first and play will continue clockwise from that player. On each turn, the player rolls all five dice at once. Any dice that show a one are worth 100 points. Any dice that show a five are worth 50 points. All other dice are not worth any points, unless there are a multiple dice showing that number. If multiple dice are showing the same number, the player gets 100 times the number on that dice. For example, if a player rolls a one, a five and three twos, they would get 100, 50 and 200 points for a total of 350 points. If the player has not scored any points, their turn is over and it is the next player's turn. However, if the player has scored points on a roll, they can decide to either keep the points and end their turn or continue to roll to try to get more points. If the player gets more points on the next roll, it is added to her total, however, if she does not get any points on her next roll, her turn is over and she loses all of her points. Have someone record the points for each round throughout the game. The first player to score 1000 points is the winner.

Penny For Your Thoughts

2 pennies of the same year for each guest
1 jar
1 prize

This game is a great icebreaker for a large group. Collect two pennies of the same year for each guest, with different years for each guest. For example, if you have 15 guests, collect 30 pennies from 15 different years. When a guest arrives to the party, give them one penny and place the penny with the corresponding year in a jar. When all the guests have arrived and have their penny, have the hostess select a penny from the jar. The person with the corresponding year penny has to tell a little about themselves and how they know the hostess. After the hostess has picked all the pennies from the jar and everyone has spoken, she places the pennies back in the jar and chooses one again from the jar. The person with the corresponding year penny wins a prize!

Guess the Spice

10 or more different spices
10 small containers
1 piece of paper for each guest
1 pencil for each guest
1 prize

Before your guests arrive, empty the spices from their original containers into 10 small containers. Label each container with a number and keep a master list for yourself of the corresponding number and name of the spice. When all the guests have arrived, have the guests sit in a circle and pass each bowl around one at a time. Tell the guests to close their eyes as you carry the bowl around the circle, giving each guest a chance to smell the spice. Tell the guests they are not allowed to look at or touch the spices. When you have finished giving each guest a chance to smell the spice, instruct them to write down their guess for the contents of the bowl. Repeat with the remaining bowls of spices. After each guest has written down a guess for all 10 spices, reveal the correct answers by reading from your master list. The guest with the most correct guesses is the winner of the prize.

Know Your Kitchen

11 sandwich bags
1/4 C. flour
1/4 C. sugar
1/4 C. salt
1/4 C. baking powder
1/4 C. baking soda
1/4 C. powdered sugar

1/4 C. cornstarch
1/4 C. cream of tartar
1/4 C. powdered milk
1/4 C. unflavored gelatin
1/4 C. Bisquick baking mix
1 prize

Before your guests arrive, fill each of the 11 sandwich bags with one of the listed ingredients. Label each bag with a number and keep a master list for yourself of the corresponding number and name of the ingredient. When all the guests have arrived, have the guests sit in a circle and pass each bag around one at a time. Tell the guests to feel the bags as they are passed around the circle, but not to smell, touch or taste the ingredient inside each bag. When each guest has had a chance to feel the bag, instruct them to write down their guess for the contents of the bag. Repeat with the remaining bags of ingredients. After each guest has written down a guess for all 10 bags, reveal the correct answers by reading from your master list. The guest with the most correct guesses is the winner of the prize.

The Purse Game

1 empty plate
4 or more players

Before your guests arrive, make a master list of 20 different items that could potentially be carried in a purse, such as a pen, a paperclip, a business card, aspirin, a receipt or a credit card. Be sure to add some odd items like a sock, a spoon or dental floss. When all the guests have arrived, have the guests sit in a circle and place the empty plate in the middle of the circle on the floor. Have each guest sit with their purse on their lap. Call out one item from your list and have each guest dig through their purse to try to find that item. The first person to find that item and place it on the plate gets 1 point. Be sure to empty off the plate before reading the next item. The player who has the most points at the end of the game is the winner of the prize.

Stealing Bundles

1 pack of cards
2 to 4 players

The object of this game is to collect the most cards to your bundle. Determine which player is the dealer. Have the dealer deal four cards, face-down, to each player. The dealer sets all remaining cards in the deck face-down in the center of the table and turns the first three cards face-up on the table. The players can pick up their cards and look at them. The first player to the left has to choose one of her four cards to place face-up on the table. If any of the 3 face-up cards match that card, the player can take the matching card and place it with her face-up card in front of her to start her "bundle". Cards match up if they are of the same number or face. For example, a Queen matches only a Queen and a 3 matches only a 3. Any matched cards acquired during the game are always stacked on top of that player's bundle, with the card last played on top as the only card visible. If that player can't match a card from the 3, she places only her face-up card in her bundle. If that player can match one of her cards with the top card of an opponent's bundle, that player can steal the other player's entire bundle and place those cards on their own bundle. Each player gets only one chance per turn to match a card or steal an opponent's bundle and then it is the next player's turn. After each player has played their four cards, the same dealer takes the remaining cards from the face-down pile and deals another four cards to each player. However, this time the dealer does not place any cards face-up. Play continues as players try to steal bundles from opposing players until all cards have been dealt and played. The player with the most cards in their own bundle is the winner.

Word Scramble

1 sheet of paper for each player
1 pencil for each player
1 stopwatch
1 prize

Before the guests arrive, on a sheet of paper, type or write out the words below to make a master list. Print one copy for yourself. Then retype or rewrite the words with the letters of each word in a scrambled order. Add more words or take words off the list as desired. Print or make copies of the scrambled words so there are enough sheets for each player to have 1 sheet of scrambled words. When all of the guests have arrived, give each player a sheet of the scrambled words and 1 pencil. Tell the players to try to unscramble as many of the words on the list as they can within 10 minutes. After 10 minutes, collect all pencils from the players and read the correct unscrambled words from your master list. The player with the most correct answers wins the prize.

- Red Hat
- Tea Party
- Entertainment
- Wear Purple
- Warning
- Summer Gloves
- Satin Sandals
- Laughter
- Over Fifty
- Queen Mother
- Silliness

Decorations

Edible Topiaries

Foam balls or cylinders
Clay pots
12" wooden dowels
Decorative moss or small rocks
Toothpicks
Various fruits and vegetables

To make a round fruit topiary, place a foam ball inside a clay pot. Insert a wooden dowel into the foam ball, so the dowel stands up straight. Pack moss or small decorative rocks tightly around the foam ball in the pot to hold the ball securely in place. Place another foam ball on the top of the dowel, making sure the dowel does not poke through the other end of the foam ball. Press toothpicks into large strawberries, raspberries and blueberries and press the other end of each toothpick into the round ball, until the ball is completely covered.

To make a cylinder vegetable topiary, place the cylinder upright on a decorative tray. If available, use a green cylinder, which is less noticeable than white. Press toothpicks into various vegetables, such as cherry tomatoes, green pepper slices, cauliflower and broccoli florets. Press the other end of each toothpick into the foam cylinder, until the cylinder is completely covered. Encourage guests to snack from the topiaries throughout the party.

Fruit Décor

12 kiwis
12 oranges
12 limes
12 lemons
1 large glass vase

    This is a very colorful and attractive centerpiece for any table. Make sure to change the water daily. Discard fruit after use in vase.

    Cut most of the kiwis, orange, limes and lemons in half. Fill a large glass vase with the cut fruit and whole fruit, arranging the fruit so the cut edges face out. If necessary, add more fruit to fill the vase completely. When the vase is full, pour water over the fruit. Arrange flowers in vase as normal, sticking stems between fruits to hold in place.

Ivy Centerpiece

Florist's foam
1 pedestal planter
Decorative moss
Toothpicks or florist's pins
1 bunch artificial ivy
Various small ornaments or seasonal decorations

Fit the florist's foam tightly into the pedestal planter, pushing the foam into place. Pour water over foam and pack the moss tightly around the foam, holding in place with toothpicks or florist's pins if necessary. Arrange the artificial ivy completely over moss, holding in place with additional florist's pins. Let the ivy fall down around the planter. Embellish the ivy with various small ornaments or charms. For a fall party, stick colorful autumn leaves into the ivy. For a Christmas party, decorate the ivy with small ornaments, or, for a fresh look, stick small spring flowers into the spaces between the ivy.

Hurricane Lamps

2 (20") pieces of heavy wire   **Sand**
Pliers   **Votive candles**
Large glass jars

Cut heavy wire into two long pieces. Place long wire pieces around top of jar, just under the screw-top part of the jar (Diagram 1). Twist together pieces of wire, to secure wire tightly around jar, with additional wire sticking out of both sides (Diagram 2). Fold pieces of wire up to form a handle and twist ends of wire securely together (Diagram 3). Fill the jars with sand and place 1 votive candle inside each jar. For an outside party, hang the jars from various tree branches. For an indoor party, hang the lamps from chandeliers or sconces. For an evening get together, use the lamps to light the way to the door.

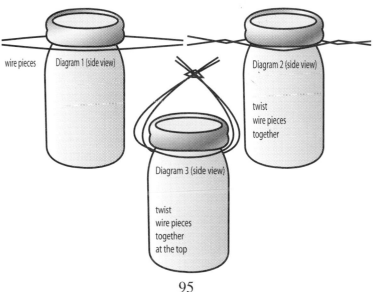

wire pieces   Diagram 1 (side view)   Diagram 2 (side view)

twist
wire pieces
together

Diagram 3 (side view)

twist
wire pieces
together
at the top

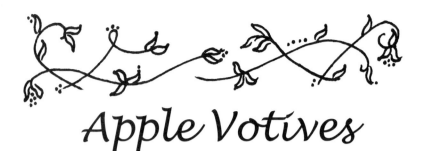

Apple Votives

6 large red apples
6 votive candles
Clear floor wax

Using an apple corer, cut the centers out of each apple, being careful not to cut through the apple completely. Cut the hole in each apple wide enough to hold 1 votive candle. Fill a large bowl with clear floor wax and dip each apple in wax. Set the apples on waxed paper, until the floor wax dries. Place one votive candle in the hole in each apple. The apples make great decorations placed on a table. Also, for a fall party, fill a large metal bucket with water and float the apple votives in the bucket.

Napkin Folding
The Classic Fold

Place the napkin on a flat surface in a large open square. Fold the square in half diagonally to make a large triangle. Fold each tip of the triangle into the center to make a smaller square (Diagram 1). Fold the two top corners of the square down to the middle to make another triangle (Diagram 2). Fold the napkin in half once more and stand on edge on each plate (Diagram 3).

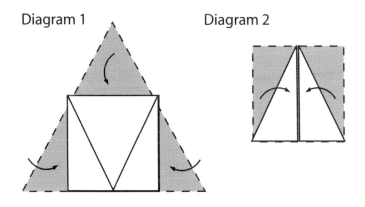

Diagram 1

Diagram 2

Diagram 3

Napkin Folding
The Pointed Hat

Place the napkin on a flat surface in a large open square. Fold the square in half to make a rectangle. Starting at one of the shorter ends of the rectangle, loosely roll the corner towards the center until a cone is formed (Diagram 1). When the napkin is completely rolled, there should be a pointed corner at the open end of the cone (Diagram 2). Fold the pointed corner up on the outside of the cone and stand cone upright on each plate (Diagram 3).

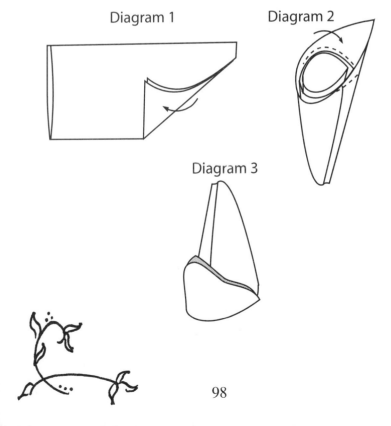

Diagram 1

Diagram 2

Diagram 3

Napkin Folding
The Open Fan

Place the napkin on a flat surface in a large open square. Fold the square in half to make a rectangle. Starting at one of the shorter end of the rectangle, make 1/2" pleats toward the center of the napkin, folding back and forth (Diagram 1). Continue to make pleats until half of the napkin has been pleated. Fold top unpleated corner down to bottom of the pleats and turn the edge under (Diagram 2). Place the napkin on each plate and lightly release the pleats to make a fan (Diagram 3).

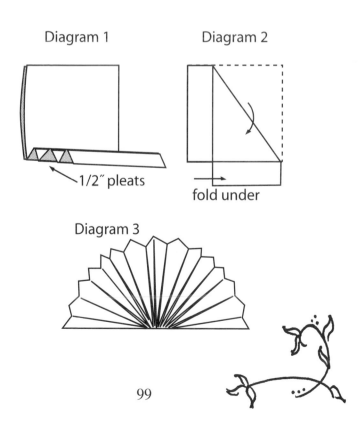

Diagram 1

1/2" pleats

Diagram 2

fold under

Diagram 3

Napkin Folding
The Simple Envelope

Place the napkin on a flat surface in a large open square. Fold the square in half diagonally to make a large triangle. Fold in the two side corners toward the middle, one at a time, ironing flat after each fold (Diagram 1). Place folded napkin on or next to each plate and tuck the cutlery into the folds of the napkin (Diagram 2).

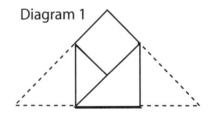

Diagram 1

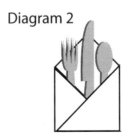

Diagram 2

Floating Gardens

Any small household plant
Glass vases
Liquid plant fertilizer

Nearly any small household plant can be used to make floating gardens. Carefully remove the plant from its pot over a large bowl. Using a fork, gently remove the dirt from the roots of the plant. Gently work the roots until all dirt has been loosened. Run the roots under water to remove any leftover dirt. The healthy roots will be nice and white. Carefully trim any brown roots from the plant, since they are dead. Fill a glass vase with distilled water and place the plant in the water. Gently mix in a few drops of liquid plant fertilizer. The plants will float in the garden. Place the small floating gardens on the table as a centerpiece or throughout your home.

No-Sew Table Runner

1 (16") wide piece of fabric
Iron
Fabric glue

A table runner is a great way to dress up any table. Use these no-sew directions to make a quick and easy table runner that will look fabulous at your next party.

Place the 16" wide piece of fabric on the table for which you are making the runner. Cut the fabric the length of the table, plus 6" on either side of the table. Turn the fabric piece over, so the right side is facing down. Fold in 1" on either long side of the fabric, so the fabric is now 14" wide. Iron down each side. Place fabric glue under the fold and press down until glue has dried. On either end of the fabric, fold the ends in 1", iron and glue down these edges. When all the glue has dried, turn the runner over so the right side faces up.

Beaded Cutlery

Thin craft wire
Cutlery
Hot glue gun with glue
Various colored beads
Wire cutter

Using one piece of cutlery at a time. Secure one end of the wire at the neck of the knife, spoon or fork with a drop of hot glue. Don't worry, the hot glue will not damage your cutlery and can be peeled off any metal. Start wrapping the thin wire around the neck of the piece of cutlery about 10 times. String a few beads onto the wire and wrap the wire again around the cutlery. Do this 5 more times, adding a few beads each time you wrap around the knife, spoon or fork. Using a wire cutter, cut the end of the wire and secure the wire at the back of the cutlery with another drop of hot glue.

Floral Candles

Long white taper candles
Short stemmed flowers*
Thin craft wire
Wire cutter
1/4" wide satin ribbon

Cut the stems of each flower to equal lengths, about 2" long. Using your hands, arrange the flowers in a ring around each taper candle, about 4" or 5" from the top of the candle. Carefully wrap thin craft wire around the candles to hold the stems in place, being careful not to cut through the stems with the wire. Twist the end of the wire together to hold the flowers in place. Wrap a piece of satin ribbon around the flower stems to cover the wire and tie a bow to secure the ribbon. Cut the ends of the ribbon at a slant. Place taper candles in candle holders and place on table for a centerpiece.

*Use small flowers such as pansies, lavender, small chrysanthemums and sugar snap peas.

Party Favors

Easy Red Party Favor Bags

Makes 4 (9"x9") bags

1 yard of 45" red fabric
Pinking shears
Thread to match fabric
Candy or small gifts to fill bag
1 1/2 yards ribbon or lace per bag

Iron the fabric piece and lay fabric flat on the floor. Cut the fabric into four 10"x19" pieces (Diagram 1), using pinking shears to avoid fraying. Fold each of the four fabric rectangles together, right sides facing, at the fold line. Sew 1/4" seams on both sides of each bag (Diagram 2). Turn each bag inside out and iron flat. Fill each bag with candy or other small gifts. Tie each bag closed using the decorative ribbon or lace.

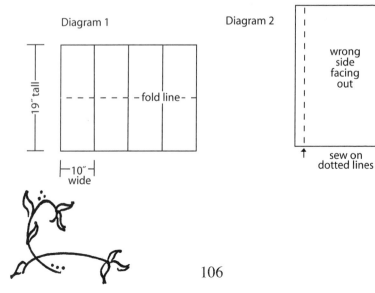

Diagram 1

19" tall

— — — — fold line — — —

⊢10"⊣
wide

Diagram 2

wrong
side
facing
out

↑ sew on ↑
dotted lines

Homemade Wine Charms

Makes 4 wine charms

30 to 40 small beads
4 small charms*
4 wine charms rings or 20" jewelry wire
Needle nosed pliers

String beads and charms onto premade wine charm rings (available at most craft stores). Follow direction on premade rings by connecting the two ends with pliers. If using jewelry wire, bend 4 1/2" lengths of wire into a U-shape and string beads and charms onto wire (Diagram 1). Bend each end of the wire in the opposite direction (Diagram 2) and hook together. Let each guest choose which charm they would like around the base of their wine or cocktail glass.
*Try to find charms that are appropriate to the occasion. For example, use holiday themed charms for a holiday party.

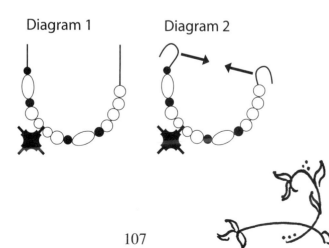

Diagram 1   Diagram 2

Bell Card Holders

Makes 4 place cards

4 small bells with handles
4 key rings
Ribbon
Card stock paper
Metallic pen

Attach one key ring to the top handle of each bell. Arrange the ring so it stands up straight. Tie a small piece of ribbon around the key ring on each bell into a bow. Cut the card stock into four small rectangles and write the names of one guest on each rectangle with the metallic pen. Or use the place card templates on page 118 by photocopying the cards onto heavy paper. Slip the name card in between the rings of the key ring to hold in place. Place each name card at the desired place setting on your table.

Mini Pot Place Cards

Makes 4 place cards

4 mini terra cotta flower pots
Colored chalk
Hair spray
4 small fresh flowers
4 small floral tubes

Wash mini terra cotta flower pots and let dry thoroughly. Write the name of one guest on each flower pot with colored chalk, with the bottom of the pot being the top side. Decorate mini flower pots further with chalk by drawing small flowers or other designs. Lightly spray hair spray over colored chalk on pots and let dry. Turn pots upside down on table and insert one small flower into the hole in the bottom of each pot. Fill small floral tubes with water and gently slip the stem of each flower into a floral tube underneath each pot to keep flowers fresh throughout the day. Place each pot place card at the desired place setting on your table.

Red Hat Candy Cups

Red or white cupcake paper liners
Red paper
Stapler
Scissors
Nuts and/or candy

For each guest, photocopy or cut out and trace the template from the bottom of the page onto red paper. Cut out the hat images from the paper, making sure there is one red hat for each guest. Staple one red paper hat onto each cupcake liner so the hat stands up against the side of the paper liner. Fill each cup with nuts and/or candy and set one filled cup at each place setting on the table.

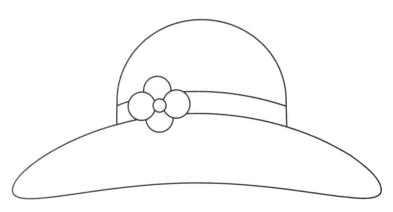

Wrapped Apples

Makes 4 favors

4 apples or oranges
4 (10") square sheets of red crepe paper
Purple ribbon
Black felt tip pen

To make each favor, place 1 apple or orange in the center of each red crepe paper square. Wrap the crepe paper up and around the apple and gather at the top and twist. Tie a piece of purple ribbon into a bow around the top of each wrapped apple. Fan out the top of the crepe paper. Using the felt tip pen, carefully write the name of each guest onto the paper around each apple. Place each wrapped apple at the desired place setting on your table.

Shell Candles

Short lengths or candle wick
Empty oyster shells
Florist's clay
Wooden toothpicks
Leftover ends of candles

To make each candle, attach one end of each candle wick length into the bottom of each empty oyster shell with florist's clay. Tie the remaining end of each wick around one toothpick so the wick is held taught. Rest the end of the toothpick on the edges of the shell so the wick is held upright in each shell. In a double boiler over medium high heat, place leftover ends of candles and heat until candles are melted to liquid wax. Discard any pieces of wick and carefully pour the hot wax into each empty oyster shell. Set aside the shells until the wax is completely hardened. If hollow spots will have formed in the dried wax in the shells, melt more wax and pour into shells to fill the hollow spots. When the wax has hardened completely, trim the wicks to within 1/4" of the top of the wax and light.

Take-Home Tea Bags

Markers, crayons or colored pens
Small lunch bags
Various small gifts
Stapler
10" lengths of yarn
Decorative paper

Using markers, crayons or colored pens, decorate the front of each lunch bag to look like the packet of a tea bag. Fill the bag with various goodies, such as tea bags, candy, a poem, chocolate spoons from page 115, etc. Fold over the top of each bag 2" and staple closed. Attach one end of the length of yarn within the stapled portion. From the decorative paper, cut out 2" square pieces of paper. Write the name of each guest on one small square of paper and attach to the other end of the yarn with another staple. The bag should look like a large tea bag that is full of goodies for your guests to take home with them.

Party Favor Poppers

Makes 4 poppers

4 empty toilet paper cardboard tubes
Various small gifts
Red or purple tissue paper
Decorative ribbon

Clean off empty cardboard tubes of any remaining paper or glue. If you can't find empty toilet paper tubes, cut a paper towel tube in half or cut an empty gift wrap tube into 4" sections. Wrap tissue paper around the tube by rolling lengthwise. Tie off one end of the tissue paper with decorative ribbon. Fill the open end of the tube with various goodies, such as chocolate coins, small charms or other small gifts. Tie off the remaining open end of the tube with another piece of decorative paper. At the party, give the filled poppers to your guests and have them pull on the paper at both ends of the tubes at the same time. The tearing paper should make a popping noise and the small gifts will be revealed.

Chocolate Spoons

White or semisweet chocolate bars
Plastic spoons
Colored sugar
Plastic bags
Decorative ribbon

In a double boiler over medium high heat, place chocolate bars. Heat chocolate until completely melted. Dip the plastic spoons into the melted chocolate, just to cover the end of each spoon. Place the spoons on waxed paper and sprinkle colored sugar over the chocolate. Let spoons sit until chocolate is hardened. Cover the chocolate end of each spoon with a plastic bag and tie decorative ribbon around the end of the bag to secure the bag to the spoon. Give chocolate covered spoons to each guest and encourage them to use the spoons to stir their tea or other hot drink to add a smooth chocolate flavor.

Mardi Gras Masks

Heavy weight paper   **Glue**
Paper punch   **Glitter**
Lengths or yarn or string   **Sequins**
Markers

Photocopy or cut out and trace the template on the next page onto heavy weight paper for each guest. When each guest arrives, have them cut out the mask from the paper. Using a paper punch, make a hole in either side of the mask where indicated. Encourage guests to decorate their own masks with markers, glitter and sequins – the more extravagant the better! Complete the Mardi Gras theme by passing out beads to all your guests to wear with their masks!

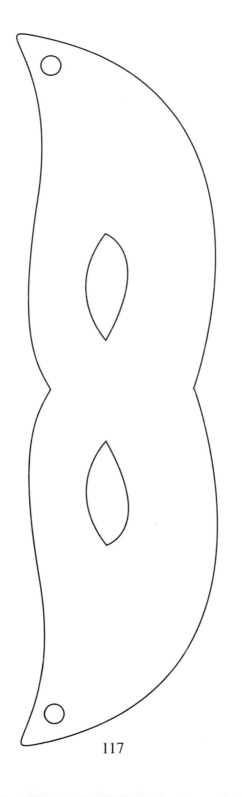

117

Templates for Bell Card Holders on page 108.

Index

Beverages

Hors d'oeuvres

Desserts

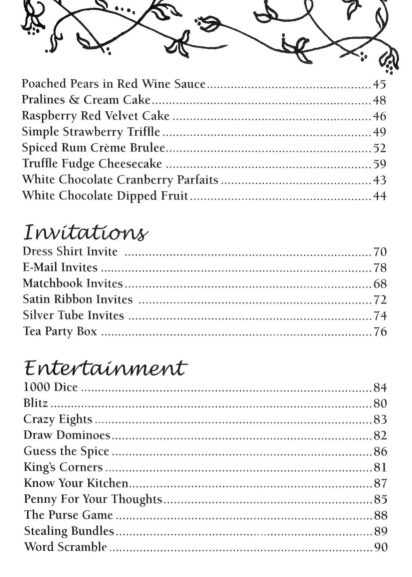

Decorations

Party Favors